Code 4386-23, No. 3, Broadman Supplies, Nashville, Tenn. Printed in USA

The Existence of God and the Beginning of the Universe

The Existence of God and the Beginning of the Universe

William Lane Craig, Ph.D.

HERE'S LIFE PUBLISHERS, INC.
San Bernardino, CA. 92402

THE EXISTENCE OF GOD AND THE BEGINNING OF THE UNIVERSE

by William Lane Craig

International Standard Book Number: 0-89840-005-8
Here's Life Publishers, Inc., Product Number: 95-014-7
Library of Congress Catalog Card Number: 79-89025

Here's Life Publishers, Inc.
P.O. Box 1576, San Bernardino, CA 92402

Scripture quotations not otherwise identified are from the Revised Standard Version of the Bible.

The author and publisher express appreciation to Celestron International for permission to reproduce its color photos of outer space.

For my brother

We may be in the universe as dogs
and cats are in our libraries,
seeing the books and hearing the
conversation, but having no inkling
of the meaning of it all.

William James, *Pluralistic Universe*

The heavens are telling the glory of
God; and the firmament proclaims
His handiwork.

Psalm 19:1 (RSV)

CONTENTS

PREFACE

This is a book for those who do not believe in God. It is my hope that this work will be the means by which some person seeking to know the truth about the universe will come to know its creator.

Several years of philosophical and scientific research have convinced me that belief in the existence of God is the most intellectually respectable position available to a person today. In this work I have tried to marshal briefly and convincingly some of the evidence in support of the thesis that God exists. Though I have written this book on a popular, easy-to-understand level, I have tried not to sacrifice anything in terms of scholarship or accuracy. Those who wish to pursue more deeply some of the issues I discuss should consult my technical study, The Kalām Cosmological Argument (London: Macmillan, 1979; New York: Barnes & Noble, 1979).

There is a danger in this sort of book that ought to be mentioned at the outset. One might receive the impression that belief in God is based solely on rational proofs, so that a person who does not find the arguments convincing can dismiss God without another thought. This would be a grave mistake. The Bible does teach that there is evidence of God's existence in the natural world around us — but it also teaches that God's Spirit "speaks" inwardly to the soul of each man in an unmistakable way, drawing him to God.

9

Because God wants all men to come to a personal knowledge of Himself, He has not abandoned man to his own ingenuity to work out by arguments alone whether God exists. Rather, God gives undeniable testimony of His existence to each individual through this inner drawing of His Spirit. The man who desires to know God will respond to this drawing; the man who is apathetic or hostile toward God will not be coerced by it.

I know that God exists because, in 1965, I responded to the inner pull of His Spirit and gave my life to Jesus Christ. Now God's Spirit lives within me and undeniably assures me of His existence. God will speak to your heart as well, giving you assurance of His presence, if you seek Him sincerely.

In this book I will share with you several arguments which I consider convincing in an attempt to show you that God exists. Should my arguments seem weak and unconvincing to you, that is my fault, not God's. It only shows that I am a poor philosopher, not that God does not exist. Whether you judge my arguments to be sound or fallacious, God still exists; He loves you and holds you accountable. I will do my best to present sound arguments to you. But ultimately you must deal, not with arguments, but with God Himself.

CHAPTER

1

Life and the Universe Without God: What Does It Really Mean?

Does God exist? Before we can even begin to answer that question, we need to gain a clear understanding of the alternative answers and their implications. For, logically, either God exists, or He does not, and the one answer means something far different from the other.

If God does not exist, life can be considered absurd. If there is no God, man inevitably is doomed to death. Like all biological organisms, he must die, and with no hope of immortality, his life leads no further than the grave. An individual's life is but a spark in the infinite blackness; it appears, flickers and dies forever. Compared to the infinite stretch of time, the span of a man's life is but an infinitesimal moment, and yet this is all the life he will ever know.

All men must come face to face with what theologian Paul Tillich has called "the threat of non-being." Though I know now that I exist, I also know that someday I will no longer exist, that I will die. This thought is staggering and threatening: to think that the person I call "myself" or "me," the person which today is so obviously alive, will someday be no more.

I remember vividly the first time my father told me as a youngster that someday I would die. When he told me, I was filled with fear and unbearable sadness. Somehow as a child the

Life and the Universe Without God: What Does It Really Mean?

13

thought just never had occurred to me. Though he tried to reassure me that this death was a long way off, that did not seem to matter. Sooner or later I would die and be no more, and that undeniable fact overwhelmed me.

Eventually I simply grew to accept the fact, as we all do. We all must learn to live with the inevitable. But the child's insight remains true: Whether it comes sooner or later, the prospect of death and the threat of non-being is a terrible horror. Man's life is just a momentary transition out of oblivion into oblivion.

Life and the Universe Without God: What Does It Really Mean?

The universe, too, faces death. Scientists tell us the universe is expanding, and everything in it is growing farther and farther apart. As it does so, it grows colder and colder, and its energy is used up. Eventually all the stars will burn out, and all matter will collapse into dead stars and black holes. There will be no light, no heat, no life — only the corpses of dead stars and galaxies ever expanding into the endless darkness and the cold recesses of space, a universe in ruins.

If there is no God, if our fate is sealed and we are awaiting an unavoidable execution, how can our lives be anything but absurd? Without God and immortality, the life we have is without ultimate significance, value or purpose. Let's look at each of these.

First, life holds no ultimate significance. If each individual passes out of existence when he dies, what ultimate significance can be assigned to his life? Does it really matter whether he ever existed at all?

It might be said that his life held importance

because it influenced others or affected the course of history. But this gives only a relative significance to his life, not an ultimate significance. His life may be important relative to other people and to certain events, but those people and events are insignificant, ultimately, since they, too, are headed for non-existence. All of history and its events and persons are meaningless, so what ultimate significance lies in influencing any of them?

The contributions of the scientist to the advance of human knowledge, the research of the doctor to alleviate pain and suffering, the efforts of the diplomat to secure peace in the world, the sacrifices of good men everywhere to better the lot of the human race — all these come to nothing. In the end they do not make one bit of difference. They cannot make less dark or less final the oblivion we all must enter. So our lives ultimately are meaningless, and the activities with which we fill those lives are equally meaningless.

Look at it from another perspective: Scientists say that the universe originated in an explosion called the "big bang" about 15 billion years ago. Suppose the big bang had never occurred, and the universe had never existed. Would that make any difference in the long run? The universe will die anyway; in the end it will not matter that it ever even existed. Therefore it is without ultimate significance.

The same is true of the human race. Mankind is a doomed race in a dying universe. Since it will eventually cease to exist, it makes no ultimate

Life and the Universe Without God: What Does It Really Mean?

difference whether it ever did exist. Mankind cannot be more significant than a swarm of mosquitoes or a barnyard of pigs, if their end is all the same. The same blind cosmic process that coughed them up in the first place will eventually swallow them all up again. This is the horror of modern man: Because he ends in nothing, he *is* nothing.

It is important at this point to realize that man needs more than immortality in order for life to hold meaning. Mere duration of existence does not make that existence meaningful. Man and the universe could exist forever, but without God to define and order that existence, they could still claim no ultimate significance. Such an unending and unexplained existence would, in a way, be worse than oblivion.

To illustrate: I once read a science-fiction story in which an astronaut became marooned on a barren chunk of rock lost in outer space. He had with him two vials: one containing poison and the other a potion that would make him live forever. Realizing his predicament, he gulped down the poison, but to his horror, he discovered he had swallowed the wrong vial. He had taken the potion for immortality; he was cursed to exist forever, to live a life without meaning and without end.

If life is to hold ultimate significance, man needs more than immortality; he needs God to define and order and give meaning to that immortality. But if God does not exist, he has neither, and life itself is without ultimate significance.

Life and the Universe Without God: What Does It Really Mean?

16

Second, life holds no value. If all life ends at the grave, it makes no difference whether one lives as a Stalin or as a saint. The Russian writer Fyodor Dostoyevsky put it thus: "If there is no immortality, then all things are permitted."[1]

On this basis, a writer like Ayn Rand is absolutely correct to praise the "virtues" of selfishness. Live totally for self; no one holds you accountable. Indeed, it would be foolish to do otherwise, for life is too short to jeopardize it by acting out of anything but pure self-interest. Sacrifice for another person would be stupid.

But the problem becomes even more complex. For even given an assurance of immortality, if there is no God, there can be no absolute standards of right and wrong. We are reduced to the bare, valueless fact of existence in an indifferent universe. The concept of morality loses all meaning in a world without God. It becomes impossible to condemn war, oppression or crime as evil. Nor can one praise brotherhood, equality or love as good. Without God, no one can say that you are right and I am wrong; good and evil do not exist.

Third, life is without purpose. If death stands with open arms at the end of life's trail, then what is the goal of life? There is no ultimate reason for man's life.

In the last half of the 20th century, man seems to be faced with the imminent prospect of nuclear holocaust or worldwide famine. We may have finally reached the end of our rope, and our destruction is being pronounced, not by prophets of doom, but by intelligent persons in the scientific community.

Life and the Universe Without God: What Does It Really Mean?

17

*Life
and the
Universe
Without
God:
What
Does It
Really
Mean?*

Shortly before his death, Mao Tse-Tung met personally with Henry Kissinger and delivered to him what Kissinger described as the most brilliant and cold-blooded analysis of the world's future: Nuclear war will wipe out most of the world's population, and out of the ashes the remnant of the Chinese proletariat will arise and dominate the earth. One must ask, though, to what end will they have survived? Is there a purpose for the human race, or will it simply peter out someday, lost in the oblivion of an indifferent universe?

The English writer H. G. Wells foresaw such a prospect. In his novel *The Time Machine*, Wells' time traveller journeys far into the future to discover the destiny of man. What he finds is a dead earth, save for a few lichens and moss, orbiting a gigantic red sun. The only sounds are the rush of the wind and the gentle ripple of the sea. "Beyond these lifeless sounds," writes Wells, "the world was silent. Silent? It would be hard to convey the stillness of it. All the sounds of men, the bleating of sheep, the cries of birds, the hum of insects, the stir that makes the background of our lives — all that was over. . . ."[2] And so Wells' time traveller returned. But to what? — merely an earlier point on the purposeless rush toward oblivion.

When I first read Wells' book, I thought, "No, no! It can't end that way!" But if there is no God, it *will* end that way, like it or not. That is reality in a universe without God. It reminds me of T. S. Eliot's haunting lines:

> This is the way the world ends
> This is the way the world ends
> This is the way the world ends
> Not with a bang but a whimper.[3]

What is true of mankind as a whole is true of each of us individually: we are here to no purpose. Our lives are not qualitatively different from that of a dog. I know that is harsh, but it is true. The ancient writer of Ecclesiastes put it this way: "The fate of the sons of men and the fate of beasts is the same; as one dies, so dies the other. . . . All go to one place; all are from the dust, and all turn to dust again."[4] This book from the Bible reads like a piece of modern existentialistic literature in which the writer shows the futility of pleasure, wealth, education, political fame and honor in a life whose end is death.

Life and the Universe Without God: What Does It Really Mean?

But even if life did not end in death, it would still be without purpose if God does not exist. For then man and the universe would simply be accidents of chance, thrust into existence for no reason. With no creator, the universe is a cosmic accident, a chance explosion. It exists for no reason.

And man is a freak of nature — a blind product of matter plus time plus chance. He is no more than a lump of slime that evolved rationality, and he has no more purpose in life than a species of insect, for both are the result of the blind interaction of chance and necessity.

The late French molecular biologist Jacques Monod proclaimed:

> Chance alone is at the source of all novelty, all creation in the bio-sphere. Pure chance, only

19

chance, absolute but blind liberty at the root of the prodigious edifice that is evolution: this central notion of modern biology is today no longer just a hypothesis among the possible . . . hypotheses. . . . The idea of chance is the only one compatible with the facts of observation and experience. . . . Man finally knows that he is alone in the indifferent immensity of the universe.[5]

Life and the Universe Without God: What Does It Really Mean?

One philosopher said, ". . . Human life is mounted upon a subhuman pedestal and must shift for itself alone in the heart of a silent and mindless universe."[6]

What is true of the universe and of man in general is also true of us as individuals. We appear to be the result of a combination of factors of heredity and environment, the victims of a genetic and environmental roulette. Psychologists following Sigmund Freud tell us our actions are the result of various repressed sexual tendencies. Sociologists like B. F. Skinner argue that all our choices are determined by conditioning, that our freedom is an illusion. Biologists like Francis Crick regard man as an electro-chemical machine, which can be controlled by altering the genetic code. In any case, without God the creator in the picture, you become nothing more than a miscarriage of nature, thrust into a purposeless universe to live a purposeless life.

Perhaps the best summary of modern man's predicament is the moving words of MIT physicist Steven Weinberg at the conclusion of his much acclaimed book, *The First Three Minutes:*

However all these problems may be solved, and whichever cosmological model proves correct, there is not much comfort in any of this. It is almost irresistable for humans to believe that we have some special relation to the universe, that human life is not just a more-or-less farcical outcome of a chain of accidents reaching back to the first three minutes, but that somehow we were built in from the beginning. As I write this I happen to be in an airplane at 30,000 feet, flying over Wyoming en route from San Francisco to Boston. Below the earth looks very soft and comfortable — fluffy clouds here and there, snow turning pink as the sun sets, roads stretching straight across the country from one town to another. It is very hard to realize that this is all just a tiny part of an overwhelmingly hostile universe. It is even harder to realize that this present universe has evolved from an unspeakably unfamiliar early condition, and faces a future extinction of endless cold or intolerable heat. The more the universe seems comprehensible, the more it also seems pointless.

Life and the Universe Without God: What Does It Really Mean?

But if there is no solace in the fruits of our research, there is at least some consolation in the research itself. Men and women are not content to comfort themselves with tales of gods and giants, or to confine their thoughts to the daily affairs of life; they also build telescopes and satellites and accelerators and sit at their desks for endless hours working out the meaning of the data they gather. The effort to understand the universe is one of the very few things that lifts human life a little above the level of farce, and gives it some of the grace of tragedy. [7]

The pathos of these words requires no comment. Banish God from the universe, and Weinberg is absolutely correct. Trapped in a life without ultimate significance, value or purpose, man's genius only serves to make his situation all the more tragic. This is hollow consolation.

I hope you begin to understand the gravity of the alternatives before us. As one modern writer phrased it, "If God is dead, then man is dead, too."[8] This is why the question of the existence of God is so vital to man.

Life and the Universe Without God: What Does It Really Mean?

Someone might say, "Then we have no recourse but simply to accept the absurdity of the universe bravely and get on with the business of living." The problem is that man cannot live consistently with such an atheistic world view.

Francis Schaeffer has explained this well.[9] Modern man, says Schaeffer, lives in a two-story universe. The lower story is the finite world without God, where life is absurd. Modern man lives in the lower story because he believes there is no God. In the upper story we find God, and with Him, meaning, value and purpose.

Modern man's problem is that he cannot live in the lower story, where life is absurd. So he continually makes leaps of faith into the upper story to affirm meaning, value and purpose. But he has no right to make such a leap; to do so is totally inconsistent because these values cannot exist without God, and man in the lower story does not have God.

Let's look again at the three areas in which life without God falls short and take a look at modern man's failure to live consistently with his denial of God.

First, the area of significance. Without God,

life can have no meaning, yet philosophers continue to live as though life does have meaning. Jean Paul Sartre, for example, argues that one may create meaning for his life by freely choosing to follow a certain course of action. Sartre chose Marxism.

Now such a program is utterly inconsistent. One cannot say that life is absurd and then, in the same breath, claim that one can create meaning for his life. A man trapped in the lower story where life is absurd has no basis for a leap into the upper story where life has meaning. For the lower-story man who has no God there can be no meaning in life.

Life and the Universe Without God: What Does It Really Mean?

Sartre's program is actually an exercise in self-delusion. It is easy to see that the universe does not really acquire meaning just because I give it one, for suppose I give the universe one meaning and you give it another. Who is right? The answer, of course, is neither one. The universe without meaning remains meaningless, no matter how we regard it, just as the earth remains round, even though someone might think it is flat. Sartre is really saying, "Let's *pretend* the universe has meaning."

Let's turn now to the problem of value, where the most blatant inconsistencies occur. First of all, atheistic humanists continue to adhere to values of love and brotherhood. Albert Camus has been rightly criticized for holding both to the absurdity of life and the ethics of human love and brotherhood. The two are logically incompatible.

Bertrand Russell was guilty of the same inconsistency. Though he was an atheist, he was

23

*Life
and the
Universe
Without
God:
What
Does It
Really
Mean?*

also an outspoken social critic, denouncing war and restrictions on sexual freedom.

To deny the existence of God is to deny the existence of absolute right and wrong. The man who lives in the lower story must logically conclude that "all things are permitted," as Dostoyevsky said. But Dostoyevsky also illustrated that man cannot live with such a view. In his novel *Crime and Punishment*, a young atheist brutally murders an old woman. He knows that, according to his presuppositions, he should not feel guilty; nevertheless, he is consumed with guilt until he confesses his crime and gives his life to God.

In *The Brothers Karamazov*, another masterpiece, Dostoyevsky tells of a man who murders his father because he comes to believe his brother Ivan, who claims that God does not exist and that there are no absolutes. The man then accuses Ivan himself of murdering their father, since it was Ivan who said that values do not exist. When Ivan protests, his brother cries, "So you lied! You do believe in God after all!" Unable to face the logical conclusions of his own system of beliefs, Ivan suffers a mental breakdown.

Man cannot live without values. He cannot live as though it is perfectly all right for soldiers to slaughter innocent children, as though it is just for dictatorial regimes to follow a systematic program of physical torture of political prisoners, as though it is acceptable for a man like Idi Amin to ruthlessly exterminate thousands of his own countrymen. Everything in man cries out that these acts are wrong — really wrong. But if there is no God, he has no grounds for such a cry. So he makes a leap of faith and affirms values anyway. But, in doing so, he reveals the inadequacy of a world without God.

A second problem is that, apart from the existence of God and immortality, all the evil acts of men will go unpunished and the sacrifices of good men will go unrewarded.

Richard Wurmbrand, who has been tortured for his faith in Communist prisons, says,

Life and the Universe Without God: What Does It Really Mean?

> The cruelty of atheism is hard to believe when man has no faith in the reward of good or the punishment of evil. There is no reason to be human. There is no restraint from the depths of evil which is in man. The Communist torturers often said, "There is no God, no hereafter, no punishment for evil. We can do what we wish." I have heard one torturer even say, "I thank God, in whom I don't believe, that I have lived to this hour when I can express all the evil in my heart." He expressed it in unbelievable brutality and torture inflicted on prisoners. [10]

The English theologian, Cardinal Newman, once said that if he believed that all the evils and injustices of life throughout history were not to be made right by God in the afterlife — "Why, I think I should go mad!" Rightly so. Facing a universe without moral accountability and devoid of value is unimaginably terrible. One will probably never find an atheist who lives consistently with his beliefs.

Finally, let's look at the problem of purpose in life. Most people who deny purpose in life live happily either by making up some purpose —

which amounts to self-delusion as we saw with Sartre — or by not carrying their view out to its logical conclusions.

Take the problem of death, for example. According to Ernest Bloch, modern man lives in the face of death by subconsciously borrowing his forefather's belief in immortality, even though he himself is an atheist and has no basis for such a belief. As Bloch points out, the belief that life ends in nothing is hardly "sufficient to keep the head high and to work as if there were no end."[11] By borrowing the remnants of a belief in immortality, writes Bloch,

> . . . Modern man does not feel the chasm that unceasingly surrounds him and that will certainly engulf him at last. Through these remnants, he saves . . . his sense of self-identity. Through them the impression arises that man is not perishing, but only that one day the world has the whim no longer to appear to him. Thus, . . . this quite shallow courage feasts on a borrowed credit card. It lives from earlier hopes and the support that they once had provided.[12]

But man no longer has any right to that support, since he rejects God. But in order to live purposefully, he leaps into the upper story to affirm a reason for living.

We often find the same inconsistency among those who claim that man and the universe are without reason or purpose but just came to exist by chance. Unable to live in an impersonal universe governed by blind chance, these people begin to ascribe personality and motives to the physical processes themselves. This type of leap

Life and the Universe Without God: What Does It Really Mean?

The Church of Christ
Tuscumbia, Alabama

from the lower to the upper story produces a rather bizarre manner of speech.

For example, the brilliant Russian physicists Zeldovich and Novikov, in contemplating the properties of the universe, ask why Nature chose to create this sort of universe instead of another.[13] This language is quite incredible for Marxist scientists who are supposed to be atheists. "Nature" has obviously become a sort of God-substitute, filling the role and function of God.

Francis Crick also spells nature with a capital "N" and speaks of natural selection as being "clever" and as "thinking" of what it will do.[14]

Fred Hoyle, the English astronomer, attributes to the universe itself the qualities of God.[15]

Though all these men deny the existence of God, they smuggle in a God-substitute through the back door because they cannot bear to live in a universe where everything is the chance result of impersonal forces. And it is interesting to watch them betray their views when they are pushed to their logical conclusions.

For example, proponents of women's rights are raising a storm of protest over Freudian sexual psychology, attacking it as chauvinistic and degrading to women. Some psychologists are knuckling under and revising their theories.

Now this is totally inconsistent. If Freudian psychology is really true, then it does not matter if it is degrading to women. You cannot change the truth simply because you do not like where it leads. But people cannot live consistently and happily in a world where others are devalued.

Life and the Universe Without God: What Does It Really Mean?

Life and the Universe Without God: What Does It Really Mean?

Only if God exists can a person consistently support women's rights. For if God does not exist, nobody has any value. Furthermore, natural selection dictates that the male of the species is the dominant and aggressive one, and that women have no more "rights" than a female goat or chicken. In nature, whatever is is right. But who can live with such a view? Apparently not even Freudian psychologists.

Consider the sociological behaviorism of a man like B. F. Skinner. His view leads to the sort of society envisioned by George Orwell in *1984*, where the government controls and programs the thoughts of everybody. Pavlov's dogs can be made to salivate when a bell rings, and so can human beings. If God does not exist and Skinner's theories are right, then there can be no moral objection to treating people like the rats in Skinner's rat-box as they run through their mazes, coaxed on by food and electric shocks. According to Skinner, all our actions are determined anyway. Man is not qualitatively different from a rat, since both are just matter plus time plus chance. Who can live with such a dehumanizing view?

Or finally, take the biological determinism of a man like Francis Crick. One must logically conclude that man is like any other laboratory specimen. The world was horrified when it learned of camps like Dachau, where the Nazis used prisoners for medical experiments. But why? If God does not exist, there can be no basis for objecting to the use of people as guinea pigs.

A memorial at Dachau says *"Nie Wieder"* —

"Never Again" — but this sort of thing is still going on. It was recently revealed that medical researchers in the United States had injected several people with a sterilization drug — without their knowledge or consent. This view could lead to population control whereby the weak and unwanted are killed off to make room for the strong. Must we not protest that this is wrong, that man is more than an electro-chemical machine? But the only way we can protest is if God exists. Only then can there be purpose in life.

Life and the Universe Without God: What Does It Really Mean?

Do you see why, if God is dead, man is dead, too? Man cannot live consistently as though life were ultimately without meaning, value or purpose. Friedrich Nietzsche tried, and he spent the last 10 years of his life in an insane asylum. According to his biographer, William Kaufman, Nietzsche's insanity was due in part to his atheism. The finite world alone is an insufficient base on which to maintain a happy and consistent life.

We are now thrown back to the first alternative: that God exists. This is the position of biblical Christianity. According to the Bible, God *does* exist and man's life does *not* end at the grave. God has created man with a soul which, united with a resurrection body, will live forever. All men are, in a sense, immortal, but some will inherit eternal life and others eternal death. Biblical Christianity therefore provides the two conditions necessary for a meaningful, valuable and purposeful life for man: God and immortality.

Let's look briefly at each of the three areas we examined before and sketch the biblical solution

Life and the Universe Without God: What Does It Really Mean?

to the problem. First, life has ultimate meaning and significance. Man does not cease to exist when he dies physically. Therefore, the choices he makes during this life have a real and everlasting significance. According to the Bible, man has a freedom undreamed of by the existentialists: the freedom to determine his eternal destiny. How we respond to God's offer of forgiveness in this life will determine how we spend eternity.

Not only is man in this way given everlasting existence, but he also derives significance by being created in the personal image of God. Although man as a finite being is, like the rest of the universe, utterly distinct from the infinite God (as our diagram illustrates on the left), man as a self-conscious personal being is like God and stands apart from all the rest of creation (as the right-hand side of the diagram shows):

God: infinite	God: personal
chasm	man
man	chasm
animals	animals
plants	plants
rocks	rocks

Because man is made in the personal image of God, one human being is worth more than the whole material universe. Thus, biblical Christianity affirms the significance and meaningfulness of man.

Second, life has value. Because life does not end at the grave, man is held accountable for his actions. Evil and wrong will be punished; the righteous will be vindicated. In the end, the scales of God's justice will be balanced. Every evil act committed in the universe will be punished. But for those who place their trust in Him, Jesus bears the punishment for their sins. Because God will judge the world, our actions do have genuine moral value.

Moreover, because God exists, there are absolute standards of right and wrong. The Ten Commandments are an expression of the moral nature of God Himself. God's holy and good nature is the absolute standard by which all actions are measured. Because of this we can consistently pronounce selfishness, war, hatred and oppression as truly evil. Thus biblical Christianity affirms that life has value.

Finally, third, life has purpose. Because man is given immortality, he does not simply live to die. God created us for a purpose: to be His children. I love the words of the catechism: What is the chief end of man? — to love God and enjoy Him forever. Our ultimate destiny is not the grave but the skies.

Moreover, man and the universe are not blind products of chance. God planned them from eternity, when no universe yet existed, and there was only God. Christ Himself knew before the universe ever existed that He would take on human form and die on the cross to save the men He had not yet created. Thus, man and the universe are not accidents, but the outworking of

Life and the Universe Without God: What Does It Really Mean?

31

God's eternal purpose. And we have the privilege of joining with Him as His children in accomplishing His goals. Thus, our lives are filled with purpose of eternal significance.

Life and the Universe Without God: What Does It Really Mean?

Biblical Christianity tells us, therefore, that life actually does have significance, value and purpose. Thus, man can live consistently and happily. Atheism cannot provide a world view that allows man to live consistently and happily; it leads only to despair. Biblical Christianity succeeds precisely where atheism breaks down.

Now I want to make it clear that I have not yet shown Christianity to be *true*. But I have clearly spelled out the two alternatives. If God does not exist, life is futile and absurd. If the God of the Bible does exist, then the conditions for a meaningful life are provided. Only the second alternative offers man hope of living happily and consistently. Therefore, it seems to me that, even if the evidence for these two alternatives were absolutely equal, a rational man ought to choose the latter and accept the existence of God.

Some atheists such as Anthony Flew like to talk about the "presumption of atheism" — that is, when the evidence is equal, the presumption ought to be that there is no God.

But in light of the foregoing, this seems to me completely wrong-headed. First, it is logically fallacious. Atheism is a claim to know something ("There is no God") just as much as theism ("There is a God"). Therefore, it can claim no presumption when the evidence is equal. If anything, we ought to speak of the presumption of agnosticism ("There may or may not be a God").

Second, when the evidence is equal, it seems to me only rational to accept that view which supplies significance, value and purpose to life and the universe and is therefore consistently livable. What I mean is that when the evidence is equal, it is positively irrational to prefer death, futility and destruction to life, meaningfulness and happiness. Therefore, I would be inclined to speak of the "presumption of theism." As Pascal said, we have nothing to lose and eternity to gain.

Life and the Universe Without God: What Does It Really Mean?

But, in fact, I do not think the scales are absolutely balanced. I think there are good reasons to believe that the existence of God is not only desirable but also plausible, in light of philosophical argument and scientific fact. And we shall discuss those reasons in the following chapters.

NOTES

Life and the Universe Without God: What Does It Really Mean?

1. Fyodor Dostoyevsky, *The Brothers Karamazov*, trans. C. Garnett, with a Foreword by Manuel Komroff (New York: New American Library of World Literature, Inc.; Signet Classics, 1957), bk. II, chap. 6; bk. V, chap. 5; bk. XI, chap. 8.
2. H. G. Wells, *The Time Machine* (Berkeley Publishing Corp., 1957; Berkeley Medallion Books, 1957), chap. 11.
3. T. S. Eliot, "The Hollow Men," in *The Complete Poems and Plays* (New York: Harcourt, Brace, & Co., 1934), stanza V.
4. Ecclesiastes 3:19, 20 (Revised Standard Version).
5. Jacques Monod in *Newsweek* (April 26, 1971), p. 99.
6. W. E. Hocking, *Types of Philosophy* (New York: Scribner's, 1959), p. 27.
7. Steven Weinberg, *The First Three Minutes* (London: Andre Deutsch, 1977), pp. 154,155.
8. Francis Schaeffer, *Escape from Reason* (Chicago: Inter-Varsity Press, 1968), p. 66.
9. Francis Schaeffer, *The God Who Is There* (Chicago: Inter-Varsity Press, 1968).
10. Richard Wurmbrand, *Tortured for Christ* (London: Hodder and Stoughton, 1967), p. 34.
11. Ernest Bloch, *Das Prinzip Hoffnung*, 2nd ed., 2 vols. (Frankfurt am Main: Sughkamp Verlag, 1959), 2: 360, 361.
12. *Ibid.*
13. I. D. Novikov and Ya. B. Zeldovich, "Physical Processes Near Cosmological Singularities," *Annual Review of Astronomy and Astrophysics* 11 (1973), pp. 387-410.
14. Francis Crick, "Why I Study Biology," *Washington University Magazine* (Spring, 1971), pp. 20-24.
15. Fred Hoyle, *From Stonehenge to Modern Cosmology* (San Francisco: W. H. Freeman & Co., 1972), p. 2.

CHAPTER

2

An Argument for God's Existence (1): Philosophical Proof of the Beginning of the Universe

"The first question which should rightly be asked," wrote the great German philosopher and mathematician Gottfried Wilhelm Leibniz, "is: Why is there something rather than nothing?"[1] Think about that for a moment. Why *does* anything exist at all, rather than nothing? Why does the universe, or matter, or anything at all exist, instead of just empty space?

Many great minds have been puzzled by this problem. For example, in his biography of the renowned philosopher Ludwig Wittgenstein, Norman Malcolm reports,

> . . . He said that he sometimes had a certain experience which could best be described by saying that "when I have it, I *wonder at the existence of the world.* I am then inclined to use such phrases as 'How extraordinary that anything should exist!' or 'How extraordinary that the world should exist!' "[2]

Similarly, the Australian philosopher J. J. C. Smart has said, ". . . My mind often seems to reel under the immense significance this question has for me. That anything exists at all does seem to me a matter for the deepest awe."[3]

Why *does* something exist instead of nothing? Unless we are prepared to believe that the universe simply popped into existence uncaused out

An Argument for God's Existence (1): Philosophical Proof of the Beginning of the Universe

An
Argument
for God's
Existence (1):
Philosophical
Proof
of the
Beginning
of the
Universe

of nothing, then the answer must be: Something exists because there is an eternal, uncaused being for which no further explanation is possible. But who or what is this eternal, uncaused being? Leibniz identified it with God. But many modern philosophers have identified it with the universe itself.

Now this is exactly the position of the atheist, that the universe itself is uncaused and eternal, or, as Russell remarks, ". . . The universe is just there, and that's all."[4] But this means, of course, that our lives are without ultimate significance, value or purpose, and that we are therefore abandoned to futility and despair. Indeed, Russell himself acknowledges that life can be faced only upon the "firm foundation of unyielding despair."[5]

Are there reasons to believe that the universe is not eternal and uncaused, that there is something more? I think that there are. Let's consider the universe by means of a series of logical alternatives:

Universe
beginning   no beginning
caused   not caused
personal   not personal

By proceeding through these alternatives, I think I can demonstrate how reasonable it is to believe that the universe is not eternal but had a beginning and was caused by a personal being; therefore a personal creator of the universe does exist.

The first and most crucial step to be proved in this argument is that the universe began to exist. I want to share four reasons why I believe that the universe had a beginning. First, I shall expound two philosophical arguments and second, two scientific confirmations.

Here is the first philosophical argument:

1. An actual infinite cannot exist.
2. A beginningless series of events in time is an actual infinite.
3. Therefore, a beginningless series of events in time cannot exist.

Let's first examine step one: *an actual infinite cannot exist.* I need to explain what I mean by an actual infinite. A collection of things is said to be actually infinite only if a part of it is equal to the whole of it. For example, which is greater:

$$1, 2, 3, \ldots$$
or
$$0, 1, 2, 3, \ldots ?$$

An Argument for God's Existence (1): Philosophical Proof of the Beginning of the Universe

According to prevailing mathematical thought, they are equivalent because they are both actually infinite. This seems strange because there is an extra number in one series that cannot be found in the other. But this only goes to show that in an actually infinite collection, a part of the collection is equal to the whole of the collection.

For the same reason, mathematicians state that the series of even numbers is the same size as the series of all natural numbers, even though the series of all natural numbers contains all the even numbers plus an infinite number of odd

39

numbers as well:

$$1, 2, 3, \ldots$$
$$2, 4, 6, \ldots$$

So a collection is actually infinite if a part of it equals the whole of it.

Now the concept of an *actual* infinite needs to be sharply distinguished from the concept of a *potential* infinite. A potential infinite is a collection that is increasing without limit but is at all times finite. The concept of potential infinity usually comes into play when we add to or subtract from something without stopping. Thus, a finite distance may be said to contain a potentially infinite number of smaller finite distances. This does not mean that there actually are an infinite number of parts in a finite distance; rather it means that one can keep on dividing endlessly and never reach an "infinitieth" division. Infinity merely serves as the limit to which the process approaches. Thus, a potential infinite is not truly infinite. It is simply indefinite. It is at all points finite but always increasing.

To sharpen the distinction between an actual and a potential infinite, we can draw some comparisons between them. The concept of actual infinity is used in set theory to designate a set which has an actually infinite number of members. The symbol used to designate this sort of infinity is the Hebrew letter *aleph:* א . But the concept of potential infinity finds no place in set theory, because the members of a set must be definite, whereas a potential infinite is indefinite and acquires new members as it grows. Thus, set theory has only finite or actually infinite sets.

The proper place for the concept of the potential infinite is found in mathematical analysis, as in infinitesimal calculus. There a process may be said to increase or diminish to infinity, in the sense that that process can be continued endlessly with infinity as its terminus.[6] The symbol for this sort of infinity is ∞ . The concept of actual infinity does not pertain to these operations because an infinite number of operations is never actually made.

According to the great German mathematician David Hilbert, the chief difference between an actual and a potential infinite is that a potential infinite is always something growing toward a limit of infinity, while an actual infinite is a completed totality with an actually infinite number of things.[7]

A good example contrasting these two types of infinity is the series of past, present and future events. If, as the atheist claims, the universe is eternal, then there have occurred in the past an actually infinite number of events. But from any point in the series of events, the number of future events is potentially infinite.

Thus, if we pick 1845, the birthyear of Georg Cantor, who discovered infinite sets, as our point of departure, we can see that past events constitute an actual infinity while future events constitute a potential infinity:

... past   1845   future ...

This is because the past is realized and complete, whereas the future is never fully actualized, but is always finite and always increasing. In the

An Argument for God's Existence (1): Philosophical Proof of the Beginning of the Universe

41

following discussion, it will be exceedingly important to keep the concepts of actual infinity and potential infinity distinct and not to confuse them.

A second clarification that I must make concerns the word "exist." When I say that an actual infinite cannot exist, I mean "exist in the real world" or "exist outside the mind." I am not in any way questioning the legitimacy of using the concept of actual infinity in the realm of mathematics, which is a realm of thought only. What I am arguing is that an actual infinite cannot exist in the real world of stars and planets and rocks and men.

Let me use a few examples to illustrate the absurdities that would result if an actual infinite could exist in reality. Suppose we have a library which contains an actually infinite number of books. Imagine there are only two colors of books, black and red, and these are placed on the shelves alternately: black, red, black, red and so forth. Now if somebody told us that the number of black books equals the number of red books, we would probably not be too surprised. But would we believe someone who told us that the number of black books equals the number of black books plus red books? For in this latter collection we find all the black books plus an infinite number of red books as well.

Or imagine there are three colors of books, or four or five or a hundred. Would you believe someone who claimed that there are as many books in a single color as there are in the entire collection?

An Argument for God's Existence (1): Philosophical Proof of the Beginning of the Universe

An Argument for God's Existence (1): Philosophical Proof of the Beginning of the Universe

Or imagine that there are an infinite number of colors of books. You might assume that there would be one book per color in the infinite collection. But you would be wrong. According to mathematicians, if the collection is actually infinite, there could be for each of the infinite colors an infinite number of books. So you would have an infinity of infinities. And yet it would still be true that if you took all the books of all the colors and added them together, you wouldn't have any more books than if you had taken just the books of a single color.

Let's continue. Suppose each book had a number printed on its spine. Because the collection is actually infinite, *every possible number* is printed on some book. So we could not add another book to the library, for what number would we assign to it? All the numbers have been used up! Thus, the new book could not have a number. But this is absurd, since objects in reality can be numbered.

If an infinite library could exist, it would be impossible to add another book to it. But this conclusion is obviously false, for all we have to do is tear out a page from each of the first hundred books, add a title page, stick them together and put this new book on the shelf. It would be that easy to add to the library. So the only conclusion left to us is that an actually infinite library could not exist.

But suppose we could add to the library, and I put a book on the shelf. According to mathematicians, the number of books in the collection is the same as before. How can this be? If I put the book on the shelf, there is one more book in the collection; if I take it off the shelf, there is one less. I can see myself add and remove the book. Am I really to believe that when I add the book there are no more books in the collection and when I remove it there are no fewer books? Suppose I add an infinity of books to the collection. Am I seriously to believe that there are no more books in the collection than before? What if I add an infinity of infinities of books to the collection? Is there now not one single book more in the collection than before? I find this hard to believe.

An Argument for God's Existence (1): Philosophical Proof of the Beginning of the Universe

Now let's reverse the process and loan out some of the books. Suppose we loan out book number one. Isn't there now one fewer book in the collection? Let's loan out all the odd-numbered books. We have loaned out an infinite number of books, and yet mathematicians would say there are no fewer books in the collection.

When we loaned out all these books, a great number of gaps were left behind on the shelves. Suppose we push all the books together again to close the gaps. All those gaps added together would add up to an infinite distance. But, according to mathematicians, the shelves would still be full, the same as before you loaned any out!

Now suppose we loaned out book numbers 4, 5, 6 . . . out to infinity. At a single stroke, the collection would be virtually eliminated, the shelves emptied, and the infinite library reduced to finitude. And yet, we have removed exactly the same number of books this time as when we first loaned out all the odd numbered books!

Does anybody believe such a library could exist in reality?

These examples serve to illustrate that an actual infinite cannot exist in the real world. Again I want to underline the fact that what I have argued in no way threatens the theoretical system bequeathed by Cantor to modern mathematics. Indeed, some of the most eager enthusiasts of trans-finite mathematics, such as David Hilbert, are only too ready to agree that the concept of actual infinity is an idea only and has no relation to the real world. [8] So we can conclude the first step: an actual infinite cannot exist.

The second step is: *a beginningless series of events in time is an actual infinite*. By "event" I mean something that happens. Thus, this step is concerned with change and holds that, if the series of past events or changes goes back and back and never had a beginning, then, considered all together, these events constitute an actually infinite collection.

Let me provide an example. Suppose we ask someone where a certain star came from. He replies that it came from an explosion in a star that existed before it. Then we ask, where did *that* star come from? Well, it came from another star before that. And where did that star come from? From another, previous star, and so on and so on. This series of stars would be an example of a beginningless series of events in time.

Now if the universe has existed forever, then the series of all past events taken together constitutes an actual infinite, because every event in the past was preceded by another event. Thus, the series of past events would be infinite. It would not be potentially infinite, for we have seen that the past is complete and actual; only the future can be described as a potential infinite. It seems obvious, therefore, that a beginningless series of events in time is an actual infinite.

But that brings us to our conclusion: *a beginningless series of events in time cannot exist.* We know that an actual infinite cannot exist in reality. Since a beginningless series of events in time is an actual infinite, such a series cannot exist. So the series of all past events must be finite and have a beginning. But the universe *is* the series of all events, so the universe must have had a beginning.

An Argument for God's Existence (1): Philosophical Proof of the Beginning of the Universe

Let me give you a few examples to make the point clear. We know that, if an actual infinite could exist in reality, it would be impossible to add to it. But the series of events in time is being added to every day, or at least, so it appears. If the series were actually infinite, then the number of events that have occurred up to the present moment is no greater than the number of events up to, say, 1789, or any point in the past, no matter how long ago it might be.

Take another example. Suppose Earth and Jupiter have been orbiting the sun from eternity. Suppose that it takes the Earth one year to complete one orbit, and it takes Jupiter three years to complete one orbit. So for every one orbit Jupiter completes, Earth completes three. Here is the question: If they have been orbiting from eternity, which has completed more orbits? The answer is: They are equal. Now this seems absurd,

47

since the longer they went, the farther and farther Jupiter would fall behind. How could they possibly be equal?

Or, finally, suppose we meet a man who claims to have been counting from eternity and now he is finishing: . . . $-5, -4, -3, -2, -1 -0$. Now this is impossible, for we may ask, why didn't he finish counting yesterday or the day before or even the year before? By then an infinity of time had already elapsed, so that he should have finished. The fact is we would never find anyone completing such a task because at any previous point in time he would have already finished. There would never be a point in the past at which we could find him counting at all, for he would have already finished. But if, no matter how far back in time we go, we never find him counting, then it cannot be true that he has been counting from eternity. This illustrates once more that the series of past events could not be without a beginning, for if you could not count numbers from eternity, neither could you have events from eternity.

These examples underline the absurdity of a beginningless series of events in time. Because such a series is an actual infinite, and an actual infinite cannot exist, a beginningless series of events in time cannot exist. This means that the universe began to exist, which is the point that we set out to prove.

Let's look now at the second philosophical argument for the beginning of the universe. Here it is:

1. The series of events in time is a collection formed by adding one member after another.
2. A collection formed by adding one member after another cannot be actually infinite.
3. Therefore, the series of events in time cannot be actually infinite.

An Argument for God's Existence (1): Philosophical Proof of the Beginning of the Universe

This argument does not debate the existence of an actual infinite. But it does argue that an actual infinite cannot come to exist by adding the members of a collection one after the other.

Let's look at the first step: *The series of events in time is a collection formed by adding one member after another.* This point is pretty obvious. When we consider the collection of all past events, it is clear that those events did not exist simultaneously, but they existed one after another in time. So we have one event, then another after that, then another, and so on. So when we talk about the collection of "all past events," we are talking about a collection that has been formed by adding one member after another.

The second step is the crucial one: *A collection formed by adding one member after another cannot be actually infinite.* Why? Because no matter how many members a person added to the collection, he could always add one more. Therefore he could never arrive at infinity.

Sometimes this is called the impossibility of counting to infinity. No matter how many numbers you count, you could always count one more. You would never arrive at infinity.

Or sometimes this is referred to as the im-

An
Argument
for God's
Existence (1):
Philosophical
Proof
of the
Beginning
of the
Universe

possibility of traversing the infinite. You could never cross an infinite distance. Imagine a man running up a flight of stairs and every time his foot strikes the top step, another step appears above it. It is clear that the man could run forever, but he would never cross all the steps because you could always add one more step.

Now notice that this impossibility has nothing to do with the amount of time available. The very nature of the infinite requires that it cannot be formed by adding one member after another, regardless of the amount of time available.

Thus, an infinite collection could come to exist in the real world only if all the members were created simultaneously. For example, if our library of infinite books were to exist in the real world, it would have to be created instantaneously by God. God would say, "Let there be . . .!" and the library would come into existence all at once. But forming the library by adding one book at a time would be impossible, because you would never arrive at infinity.

Therefore, our conclusion must be: *The series of events in time cannot be actually infinite.* If there were an infinite number of days prior to today, then today would never arrive. It is impossible to "cross" an infinite number of days to reach today. But, obviously, today has arrived. So we know that prior to today, there cannot have been an infinite number of days. Therefore the number of days is finite, and the universe must have had a beginning.

Contemporary philosophers have shown themselves incapable of refuting this reasoning.[9]

Thus, one of them asks:

> If an infinite series of events has preceded the present moment, how did we get to the present moment? How could we get to the present moment — where we obviously are now — if the present moment was preceded by an infinite series of events? [10]

Concluding that this difficulty has not been overcome and that the issue is still in dispute, he passes on to another subject, leaving the argument unrefuted. Similarly, another philosopher comments rather weakly, "It is difficult to show exactly what is wrong with this argument," and with that remark moves on without further ado. [11]

So we have two philosophical arguments to prove that the universe had a beginning. First, we argued that an actual infinite cannot exist. Since a beginningless universe would involve an actually infinite number of past events, the universe must have had a beginning. Second, we argued that an actually infinite collection cannot be formed by adding one member after another. Since the series of past events has been formed by adding one event after another, it cannot be infinite, and the universe must have had a beginning.

An Argument for God's Existence (1): Philosophical Proof of the Beginning of the Universe

NOTES

An Argument for God's Existence (1): Philosophical Proof of the Beginning of the Universe

1. G. W. Leibniz, "The Principles of Nature and of Grace, Based on Reason," in *Leibniz Selections*, ed. Philip P. Weiner, The Modern Student's Library (New York: Charles Scribner's Sons, 1951), p. 527.
2. Norman Malcolm, *Ludwig Wittgenstein: A Memoir* (London: Oxford University Press, 1958), p. 70.
3. J. J. C. Smart, "The Existence of God," *Church Quarterly Review* 156 (1955), p. 194.
4. Bertrand Russell and F. C. Copleston, "The Existence of God," in *The Existence of God*, ed. with an Introduction by John Hick, Problems of Philosophy Series (New York: Macmillan and Co., 1964), pp. 174,176.
5. Bertrand Russell, "A Free Man's Worship," in *Why I Am Not a Christian*, ed. Paul Edwards (New York: Simon & Schuster, 1957), p. 107.
6. See Abraham A. Fraenkel, *Abstract Set Theory*, 2nd rev. ed. (Amsterdam: North Holland Publishing Co., 1961), pp. 5,6.
7. David Hilbert, "On the Infinite," in *Philosophy of Mathematics*, ed. with an Introduction by Paul Benacerraf and Hilary Putnam (Englewood Cliffs, N.J.: Prentice-Hall, 1964), pp. 139,141.
8. *Ibid.*, p. 151.
9. For an in-depth discussion of this, see my book, *The Kalām Cosmological Argument* (London: Macmillan, 1979; New York: Barnes & Noble, 1979), Appendixes 1 and 2.

   G. J. Whitrow, Professor of Mathematics at the University of London's Imperial College of Science and Technology, has repeatedly defended a form of this argument for the beginning of the universe in his various works: "The Age of the Universe," *British Journal for the Philosophy of Science*, 5 (1954-1955), pp. 215-225; *The Natural Philosophy of Time* (London & Edinburgh: Thomas Nelson & Sons, 1961, rev. ed. forthcoming); "Reflections on the Natural Philosophy of Time," *Annals of the New York Academy of Sciences*, 138 (1967), pp.

422-432; "Time and the Universe," in *The Voices of Time,* ed. J. T. Fraser (London: Penguin Press, 1968); "Time and Cosmical Physics," *Studium Generale,* 23 (1970), pp. 224-233; *What is Time?* (London: Thames & Hudson, 1972); "On the Impossibility of an Infinite Past," *British Journal for the Philosophy of Science,* 29 (1978), pp. 39-45.

Another excellent work is Stuart Hackett, *The Resurrection of Theism* (Chicago: Moody Press, 1957).

10. John Hospers, *An Introduction to Philosophical Analysis,* 2nd ed. (London: Routledge & Kegan Paul, 1967), p. 434.

11. William L. Rowe, *The Cosmological Argument* (Princeton, N.J.: Princeton University Press, 1975), p. 122.

An Argument for God's Existence (1): Philosophical Proof of the Beginning of the Universe

CHAPTER

3

An Argument for God's Existence (2): Scientific Confirmation of the Beginning of the Universe

Some people are very skeptical about philosophical arguments. They prefer to have scientific proof of a fact. Therefore, I now want to share two scientific confirmations of the philosophical arguments I presented in the last chapter.

This evidence is drawn from remarkable discoveries made within the last 50 years in what is undoubtedly one of the most exciting and rapidly developing fields of science: astronomy and astrophysics. (Evidence of the galloping rate of research in this field may be seen in the fact that there were 54 research papers published in the *Astrophysical Journal* in 1935; but in 1975, 734 papers were published, weighing 36 pounds.) With astounding speed, one breakthrough has come upon the heels of another so that today the idea that the universe did have a beginning prevails among scientists. I contend that a universe with an absolute beginning is not only philosophically logical but also fits the scientific facts of experience.

Let's look at the first scientific confirmation: the evidence from the expansion of the universe. Prior to the 1920's, scientists assumed that the universe as a whole was stationary; it was not going anywhere. But in 1929 an astronomer named Edwin Hubble proved otherwise. Hubble observed that the light from distant galaxies

An Argument for God's Existence (2): Scientific Confirmation of the Beginning of the Universe

appeared to be redder than expected. To explain this, he argued that the universe is expanding, and the light from the stars is affected since they are moving away from us.

But this is the interesting part: Hubble showed not only that the universe is expanding but also that *it is expanding the same in all directions.* To get a picture of this, imagine a balloon with dots painted on it. As you blow up the balloon, the dots get farther and farther apart. Now those dots are just like the galaxies in space. Everything in the universe is growing farther apart. Thus the relations in the universe do not change, only the distances:

An Argument for God's Existence (2): Scientific Confirmation of the Beginning of the Universe

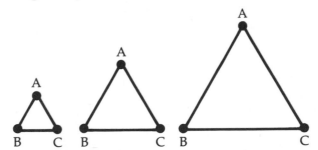

If A, B and C are three galaxies, then as the universe expands, they will grow farther and farther apart, but their relations will remain constant.

Now the staggering implication of this is that at some point in the past *the entire known universe was contracted down to a single point,* from which it has been expanding ever since. The farther back one goes in the past, the denser the universe becomes, so that one finally reaches a point of *infinite density* from which the universe began to expand. That initial event has come to be known as the "big bang."

How long ago did the big bang occur? Only during the 1970's have accurate estimates become available. In a very important series of six articles published in 1974 and 1975, the famous astronomers Allan Sandage and G. A. Tammann estimated that the big bang occurred about 15 billion years ago.[1]

Four of the world's most prominent astronomers describe that event in these words:

> The universe began from a state of infinite density. Space and time were created in that event and so was all the matter in the universe. It is not meaningful to ask what happened before the big bang; it is somewhat like asking what is north of the north pole. Similarly, it is not sensible to ask where the big bang took place. The point-universe was not an object isolated in space; it was the entire universe, and so the only answer can be that the big bang happened everywhere.[2]

This event that marked the beginning of the universe becomes all the more amazing when one reflects on the fact that a state of "infinite density" is synonymous to "nothing." No object possesses infinite density, for if it had any mass at all, it would not be *infinitely* dense.[3] Therefore, as astronomer Fred Hoyle points out, the big bang theory requires the creation of matter from nothing. This is because, as one goes back in time, he reaches a point at which, in Hoyle's words, the universe was "shrunk down to nothing at all."[4]

An Argument for God's Existence (2): Scientific Confirmation of the Beginning of the Universe

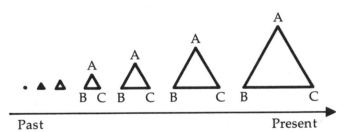

B C B C B C B C

Past   Present

An Argument for God's Existence (2): Scientific Confirmation of the Beginning of the Universe

So, according to the big bang theory, the universe had a beginning and was created out of nothing.

Some people are bothered by the idea that the universe began from nothing. To atheistic minds, such an idea is too close to the Christian doctrine of creation for comfort. But if one rejects the big bang model, he has only two alternatives: the steady state model or the oscillating model. Let's examine each of these.

According to the steady state model, the universe never had a beginning but has always existed in the same state. This model was first proposed in 1948 and has never been very convincing. According to the historian of science S. L. Jaki, this theory never secured "a single piece of experimental verification."[5] It always seemed to be trying to explain away the facts rather than explain them. According to Jaki, the proponents of this model were actually motivated by "openly anti-theological, or rather anti-Christian motivations."[6]

A second strike against this theory is the fact that a count of galaxies emitting radio waves indicates that there were once more radio sources than there are today. Therefore, the universe is not in a steady state after all.

But the real nails in the coffin for the steady state theory came in 1965, when A. A. Penzias and R. W. Wilson discovered that the entire universe is bathed with a background of microwave radiation. This radiation background indicates that the universe was once in a very hot and very dense state. But in the steady state theory, no such state could have existed, since the universe is supposed to have been the same from eternity. Virtually everyone has now abandoned the steady state model; Ivan King observed, "The steady-state theory has now been laid to rest, as a result of clear-cut observations of how things have changed with time."[7]

But what about the oscillating model of the universe? John Gribbin describes this model:

> The biggest problem with the big bang theory of the origin of the universe is philosophical — perhaps even theological — what was there before the bang? This problem alone was sufficient to give a great initial impetus to the steady state theory, but with that theory now sadly in conflict with the observations, the best way round this initial difficulty is provided by a model in which the universe expands, collapses back again, and repeats the cycle indefinitely.[8]

According to this model, the universe is sort of like a spring, expanding and contracting from eternity.

In the last three or four years, this model has been largely disproved. The key question here is whether the universe is "open" or "closed." If it is "closed," the expansion will reach a certain point, and then the force of gravity will pull

An Argument for God's Existence (2): Scientific Confirmation of the Beginning of the Universe

everything together again. But if the universe is "open," then the expansion will never stop but will go on and on forever.

Now clearly, if the universe is open, then the oscillating model is false, for the universe will never contract again. And, in fact, the scientific evidence indicates that the universe is open.

The crucial factor here is the density of the universe. According to scientific estimates, if there are more than three hydrogen atoms per cubic meter on the average throughout the universe, then the universe is closed. That may not sound like very much, but remember that most of the universe is just empty space.

I shall not go into all the technicalities of how scientists measure the density of the universe,[9] but let me simply report their conclusions. According to the evidence, the universe would have to be at least 10 times denser than it is for the universe to be closed.[10] Therefore, the universe is open by a wide margin.

Let me share with you the conclusion of Allan Sandage: (1) the universe is open; (2) the expansion will not reverse; and (3) *the universe has happened only once* and the expansion will never stop.[11]

The evidence therefore rules out the oscillating model, since it requires a closed universe. But just to drive the point home, let me add that the oscillating model of the universe is only a *theoretical* possibility, not a *real* possibility. As Dr. Tinsley of Yale has observed:

> . . . Even though the mathematics *says* that the universe oscillates, there is no known physics to

An Argument for God's Existence (2): Scientific Confirmation of the Beginning of the Universe

reverse the collapse and bounce back to a new expansion. The physics seems to say that those models start from the big bang, expand, collapse, then end.[12]

Hence, it would be impossible for the universe to oscillate from eternity. Therefore, this model is doubly impossible.

In summary then, the scientific evidence related to the expansion of the universe points to an absolute beginning of the universe about 15 billion years ago, and both the steady state and oscillating models of the universe fail to fit the facts of observational cosmology. Therefore we can conclude once more that the universe began to exist.

Now let's turn to the second scientific confirmation: the evidence from thermodynamics. According to the second law of thermodynamics, processes taking place in a closed system always tend toward a state of equilibrium. In other words, unless energy is constantly being fed into a system, the processes in the system will tend to run down and quit.

For example, if I had a bottle that was a sealed vacuum inside and I introduced into it some molecules of gas, the gas would spread itself out evenly inside the bottle. It is virtually impossible for the molecules to retreat, say, into one corner of the bottle and remain there. In fact, in a one-liter bottle of gas, the chances that 99.99% of the bottle would be filled with gas instead of the entire 100% is about $1:(10^{10})^{20}$.

This explains why the air in a room never separates suddenly into oxygen at one end and

An Argument for God's Existence (2): Scientific Confirmation of the Beginning of the Universe

nitrogen at the other. It also explains why you can step into a bath and find it pleasantly warm instead of frozen solid at one end and boiling at the other. Obviously, life would not be possible in a world where the second law of thermodynamics did not operate.

An Argument for God's Existence (2): Scientific Confirmation of the Beginning of the Universe

Now our question is, what happens when this law is applied to the universe as a whole? The universe is a gigantic closed system, since it is everything there is and there is nothing outside it.[13] This seems to imply that, given enough time, the universe and all its processes will run down and slowly grind to a halt. This is known as the heat death of the universe, and once the universe reaches this state, no further change will be possible. The universe will be dead.

Scientists recognize two possible types of heat death. If the universe is "closed," then it will die a hot death. Dr. Tinsley describes this state as follows:

> If the average density of matter in the universe is great enough, the mutual gravitational attraction between bodies will eventually slow the expansion to a halt. The universe will then contract and collapse into a hot fireball. There is no known physical mechanism that could reverse a catastrophic big crunch. Apparently, if the universe becomes dense enough, it is in for a hot death.[14]

So, if the universe is closed, it awaits a fiery death from which it will never re-emerge.

But suppose, as seems more likely, the universe is "open." Dr. Tinsley also describes the final state of this universe:

If the universe has a low density, its death will be cold. It will expand forever, at a slower and slower rate. Galaxies will turn all of their gas into stars, and the stars will burn out. Our own sun will become a cold, dead remnant, floating among the corpses of other stars in an increasingly isolated milky way.[15]

Eventually equilibrium will prevail throughout, and the entire universe will reach its final state from which no change will occur.

Now the question we must ask is: If the universe, given enough time, will reach heat death, then why is it not in a state of heat death now if it has existed forever, from eternity? If the universe had no beginning, it should now be in a state of equilibrium; its energy should be all used up.

To illustrate: My wife and I have a very loud wind-up alarm clock. If I hear the clock ticking (which is no problem, believe me), then I know that at some point in the recent past it was wound up and has been running down ever since. The universe operates the same way. Since it has not yet run down, then "In some way the universe must have been wound up,"[16] noted one baffled scientist.

Some scientists have tried to escape this conclusion; they argue that the universe oscillates back and forth from eternity and so never reaches a final state of equilibrium.

Radius of the Universe

Time

An Argument for God's Existence (2): Scientific Confirmation of the Beginning of the Universe

65

*An
Argument
for God's
Existence (2):
Scientific
Confirmation
of the
Beginning
of the
Universe*

I have already observed that such a model of the universe is a physical impossibility. But even if it were possible, the thermodynamic properties of this model imply the very beginning of the universe that its proponents seek to avoid.

For, as several scientists have pointed out, each time the model universe expands, it expands a little farther than before. If you traced those expansions back in time, you would find that they get smaller and smaller and smaller:

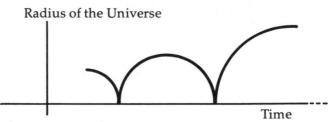

Radius of the Universe

Time

Therefore, in the words of a great Russian team of physicists from the Institute of Applied Mathematics of the U.S.S.R. Academy of Sciences, "The multicycle model has an infinite future, but only a finite past."[17] Yet another writer points out that the oscillating model of the universe still requires an origin of the universe prior to the smallest cycle.[18]

So, whether you choose a closed model, an open model, or an oscillating model, the second law of thermodynamics implies that the universe had a beginning.

Traditionally, two objections have been raised against this argument.[19] First, the argument does not work if the universe is infinite. I have two replies to this:

(a) An actually infinite universe would involve all of the counter-intuitive absurdities entailed in the existence of an actual infinite in the real world. An actually infinite universe is therefore rationally inconceivable. This is doubly true of a big-bang model, for it would require us to posit a universe approaching a state of infinite density as one regresses in the past while at the same time remaining infinite in extent.

It is often asserted that if the universe is "open," then it must be infinite. But this fails to take into consideration all of the options for the topology of space-time. For example, although a sort of saddle-shaped space-time would require an "open" and infinite universe, a model of the universe in which space-time is torus-shaped (like a doughnut) could be "open" and yet finite. Since these various theoretical topological models are equally possible, philosophical reasoning ought to incline us toward those models not entailing the counter-intuitive paradoxes involved in the existence of an actual infinite.

(b) Even if the universe were infinite, it would still come to equilibrium. As one scientist of the University of London explained in a letter to me, if every finite region of the universe came to equilibrium, then the whole universe would come to equilibrium.[20] This would be true even if there were an infinite number of finite regions. This is like saying that if every part of a fence is green, the whole fence is green, even if there are an infinite number of pickets in the fence. Since every finite region in the universe would suffer heat death, so would the entire universe.

An Argument for God's Existence (2): Scientific Confirmation of the Beginning of the Universe

The second objection is that the present state of the universe may be just a fluctuation in an overall state of equilibrium. In other words, the present energy can be likened to a ripple on the surface of a still pond.

An Argument for God's Existence (2): Scientific Confirmation of the Beginning of the Universe

Such an objection loses all sense of proportion. Fluctuations are so tiny that they are important only in systems containing a few atoms. In a universe at equilibrium, fluctuations would be imperceptible.[21] A chart showing fluctuations in the universe would be simply a straight line. So, since the present universe is in *dis*equilibrium, what are we to conclude?

According to the English scientist P. C. W. Davies, the universe must have been created a finite time ago and is now in the process of winding down.[22] He says the present disequilibrium cannot be a fluctuation from a prior state of equilibrium, since prior to this creation event, the universe simply did not exist. Thus, Davies concludes, the universe's energy "was simply 'put in' at the creation as an initial condition."[23]

In summary then, thermodynamic considerations point to a beginning of the universe, and traditional objections to this argument are unsound. Because a universe existing for infinite time could not be in the present state of disequilibrium, we must conclude, for the fourth time, that the universe began to exist.

So we now have two scientific confirmations of the beginning of the universe. The expansion of the universe, together with the fact that the universe has not yet suffered heat death, imply that the universe had a beginning.

In light of these two scientific arguments, coupled with the two philosophical arguments previously presented, I think we are amply justified in affirming the first alternative of our first disjunction: the universe had a beginning.

An Argument for God's Existence (2): Scientific Confirmation of the Beginning of the Universe

NOTES

An
Argument
for God's
Existence (2):
Scientific
Confirmation
of the
Beginning
of the
Universe

1. Allan Sandage and G. A. Tammann, "Steps Toward the Hubble Constant. I-VI," *Astrophysical Journal* 190 (1974), pp. 525-538; 191 (1974), pp. 603-621; 194 (1974), pp. 223-243, 559-568; 196 (1975), pp. 313-328; 197 (1975), pp. 265-280.

2. J. Richard Gott III, James E. Gunn, David N. Schramm, Beatrice M. Tinsley, "Will the Universe Expand Forever?" *Scientific American*, March, 1976, p. 65. This article is a popular rewrite of their article, "An Unbound Universe?" *Astrophysical Journal*, 194 (1974), pp. 543-553.

3. It is sometimes erroneously asserted in popular magazines that black holes are infinitely dense. In fact, I have read articles in *Time* and *Reader's Digest* in which black holes are said to be infinitely dense and therefore quite literally nothing! For example, *Time's* feature writer, calling black holes "parcels of nothingness," says, "The matter that formed the hole has long since disappeared, like Alice in Wonderland's Cheshire cat, leaving only the disembodied grin of its gravity." ("Those Baffling Black Holes," *Time*, Sept. 4, 1978, pp. 43,44.)

I have the sneaking suspicion that the writer has misinterpreted this statement from the *Encyclopaedia Britannica*: "Through the intense gravitational field thus set up no light could escape and the star would in effect disappear from the universe. Only its gravity would remain, like the grin of the Cheshire cat in Alice in Wonderland, and if a space traveller ran into one of these 'black holes' he too would be drawn into the same invisible kernel, there to disappear forever. . . ." (*Encyclopaedia Britannica*, 15th ed., *Propaedia*: s.v., "Matter and Energy: Introduction: The Universe of the Physicist, the Chemist and the Astronomer," by Nigel Calder.)

A black hole is so called because its intense gravity pulls in even light so that it cannot be seen; but the object itself is still there. In fact, the mass of the unseen object may be quite large, in which case its density is comparatively low.

4. Fred Hoyle, *Astronomy and Cosmology: A Modern Course* (San Francisco: W. H. Freeman & Co., 1975), p. 658.
5. Stanley L. Jaki, *Science and Creation* (Edinburgh and London: Scottish Academic Press, 1974), p. 347.
6. *Ibid.*
7. Ivan R. King, *The Universe Unfolding* (San Francisco: W. H. Freeman & Co., 1976), p. 462.
8. John Gribbin, "Oscillating Universe Bounces Back," *Nature* 259 (1976), p. 15.
9. See Gott, *et.al.*, for a good synopsis.
10. J. Richard Gott III and Martin J. Rees, "A Theory of Galaxy Formation and Clustering," *Astronomy and Astrophysics* 45 (1975), pp. 365-376; S. Michael Small, "The Scale of Galaxy Clustering and the Mean Matter Density of the Universe," *Monthly Notices of the Royal Astronomical Society*, 172 (1975), pp. 23p-26p.
11. Sandage and Tammann, "Steps Toward the Hubble Constant. VI.," p. 276; Allan Sandage, "The Redshift Distance Relation. VIII.," *Astrophysical Journal*, 202 (1975), pp. 563-582.
12. Beatrice M. Tinsley, personal letter.
13. In saying the universe is a closed system, I do not mean it is closed in the sense that its expansion will eventually contract. I rather mean that there is no energy being put into it. Thus, in the thermodynamic sense, the universe is closed, but in the sense of its density the universe is open. One must not confuse "open" and "closed" in thermodynamics with "open" and "closed" in expansion models.
14. Beatrice M. Tinsley, "From Big Bang to Eternity?" *Natural History Magazine,* October, 1975, p. 103.
15. *Ibid.*, p. 185.
16. Richard Schlegel, "Time and Thermodynamics," in *The Voices of Time,* ed. J. T. Fraser (London: Penguin Press, 1968), p. 511.
17. I. D. Novikov and Ya. B. Zeldovich, "Physical Processes Near Cosmological Singularities," *Annual Review of As-*

An Argument for God's Existence (2): Scientific Confirmation of the Beginning of the Universe

tronomy and Astrophysics, 11 (1973), pp. 401,402. See also P. C. W. Davies, *The Physics of Time Assymetry* (London: Surrey University Press, 1974), p. 188. These findings are also confirmed by P. T. Landsberg and D. Park, "Entropy in an Oscillating Universe," *Proceedings of the Royal Society of London,* A 346 (1975), pp. 485-495.

18. Gribbin, "Oscillating Universe," p. 16.
19. R. G. Swinburne, *Space and Time* (London: Macmillan, 1968), p. 304; Adolf Grunbaum, *Philosophical Problems of Space and Time,* 2nd ed., Boston Studies in the Philosophy of Science, vol. 12 (Dordrecht, Holland and Boston: D. Reidel Publishing Co., 1973), p. 262.
20. P. C. W. Davies, personal letter.
21. P. J. Zwart, *About Time* (Amsterdam and Oxford: North Holland Publishing Co., 1976), pp. 117-119.
22. Davies, *Physics,* p. 104.
23. *Ibid.*

An Argument for God's Existence (2): Scientific Confirmation of the Beginning of the Universe

ORION NEBULA

TRIFID NEBULA

ANDROMEDA

75

LAGOON NEBULA

Celestron International

VEIL NEBULA

Celestron International

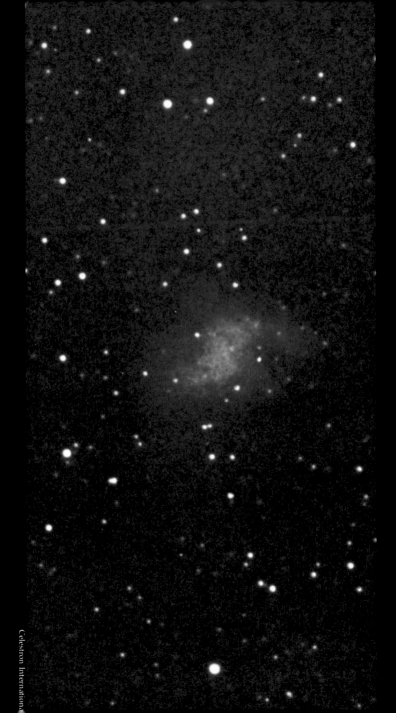

CRAB NEBULA

GLOBULAR CLUSTER

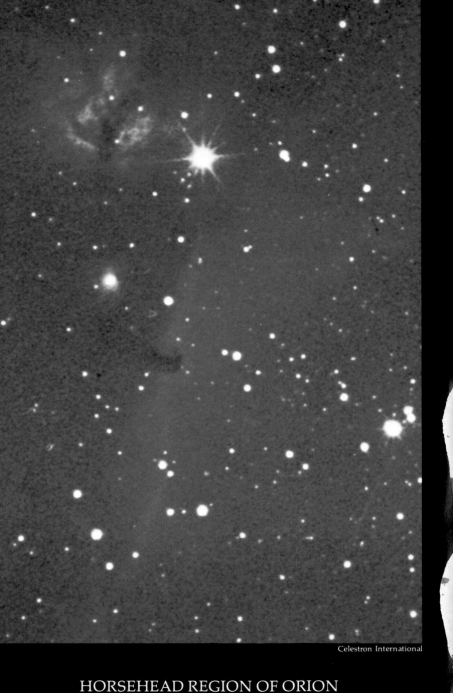

Celestron International

HORSEHEAD REGION OF ORION

4

An Argument for God's Existence (3): The Personal Creator of the Universe

Having concluded that the universe began to exist, we will now turn to our second set of alternatives: The beginning of the universe was either caused or not caused.

I am not going to give a lengthy defense of my views at this point. I do not think I need to. For probably no one in his right mind *sincerely* believes that the universe could pop into existence, uncaused, out of nothing. Even the famous skeptic David Hume admitted that it is preposterous to think anything could come into existence without a cause.[1]

This is doubly true with regard to the entire universe. As the English philosopher C. D. Broad confessed, "I cannot really *believe in* anything beginning to exist without being caused by something else which existed before and up to the moment when the thing in question began to exist."[2]

As still another philosopher has said, "It seems quite inconceivable that our universe could have sprung from an absolute void. If there is anything we find inconceivable it is that something could arise from nothing."[3] The old principle that "out of nothing, nothing comes" is so manifestly true that a sincere denial of this point is practically impossible.

Now this puts the atheist on the spot. Accord-

An Argument for God's Existence (3): The Personal Creator of the Universe

An
Argument
for God's
Existence (3):
The
Personal
Creator
of the
Universe

ing to Anthony Kenny, "A proponent of [the big bang] theory, at least if he is an atheist, must believe that the matter of the universe came from nothing and by nothing."[4] That is a pretty hard pill to swallow. In terms of sheer believability, I find it intellectually easier to believe in a God who is the cause of the universe than in a universe which popped into existence uncaused out of nothing, or in a universe which has existed from eternity without a beginning. For me, these last two positions are implausible intellectually, and it would take *more* faith for me to believe them than to believe that God exists.

At any rate, we are not dependent upon just believability, for we have already seen that both philosophical and empirical reasoning point to a beginning for the universe. So the alternatives are only two: Either the universe was caused to exist, or it sprang into existence wholly uncaused out of nothing about 15 billion years ago. The first alternative is eminently more plausible.

It is very interesting to examine the attitude of scientists toward the philosophical and theological implications of their own big bang model. Evidently there are such implications, for, as one scientist remarks, "The problem of the origin [of the universe] involves a certain metaphysical aspect which may be either appealing or revolting."[5]

Unfortunately, the man of science is, as Albert Einstein once observed, "a poor philosopher."[6] For these implications seem either to escape or not to interest most scientists.[7] Since no empirical information is available about what preceded the big bang, scientists simply ignore the issue. Thus, Hoyle, after explaining that the big bang model cannot inform us as to where matter came from or why the big bang occurred, comments, "It is not usual in present day cosmological discussions to seek an answer to this question; the question and its answer are taken to be outside the range of scientific discussion."[8]

But while this attitude may satisfy the scientist, it can never satisfy the philosopher. As one scientist admits, the big bang model only *describes* the initial conditions of the universe, but it cannot *explain* them.[9] Another astronomer concludes, "The question 'How was the matter created in the first place?' is left unanswered."[10] Thus, science begs off answering the ultimate question: Where did the universe come from? Scientific evidence points to a beginning of the universe; as rigorous scientists we may stop there and bar further inquiry, but, as thinking individuals, must we not inquire further until we arrive at the cause of the beginning of the universe?

Any unprejudiced inquirer ought to agree with me, at this point, that the universe was caused to exist. Now this is truly a remarkable conclusion. It means the universe was caused to exist by something beyond it and greater than it. This ought to fill us with awe, for it is no secret that the Bible begins with these words: "In the beginning, God created the heavens and the earth."

Now let's turn to our third set of alternatives, and I will explain why I think the cause of the

An Argument for God's Existence (3): The Personal Creator of the Universe

An Argument for God's Existence (3): The Personal Creator of the Universe

universe is personal rather than impersonal. The first event in the series of past events was, as we have seen, the beginning of the universe. We have agreed, reasonably, that that event was caused. Now the question is: If the cause of the universe is eternal, then why isn't the universe also eternal, since it is the effect of the cause?

Let me illustrate what I mean: Let's say the cause of water freezing is sub-zero temperatures. Whenever the temperature falls below zero degrees, the water freezes. Once the cause is given, the effect must follow, and if the cause exists from eternity, the effect must also exist from eternity. If the temperature were to remain below zero degrees from eternity, then any water around would be frozen from eternity. But this seems to imply that if the cause of the universe existed from eternity, the universe would also have existed from eternity. And this we know to be false.

One might say that the cause came to exist just prior to the first event. But then the cause's beginning would be the first event, and we must ask all over again for its cause. And this cannot go on forever, for we know that a beginningless series of events cannot exist. There must be an absolutely first event, before which there was no change, no previous event. We know that this first event must have been caused. Our question now is: How can a first event come to exist if the cause of that event has always existed? Why isn't the effect as eternal as the cause?

It seems to me there is only one way out of this dilemma, and that is to conclude that the cause of the universe is personal and chooses to create a universe in time. This way, God could exist changelessly from eternity but choose to create the world in time. By "choose" I do not mean God changes His mind, but that He intends to create a world with a beginning. And, therefore, a world with a beginning comes to exist. So the cause is eternal, but the effect is not. It seems to me that this is the only way the universe could have come to exist: through the will of a personal creator. And I think we are justified in calling a personal creator of the universe by the name "God."

An Argument for God's Existence (3): The Personal Creator of the Universe

I would like to make a few concluding remarks on God's relationship to time. Many people say God is outside time. But this is not what the Bible says. According to James Barr, in his book, *Biblical Words for Time*, the Bible does not make it clear whether God is eternal in the sense that He is outside time, or whether He is eternal in the sense of being everlasting throughout all time.[11] So the issue must be decided philosophically.

Prior to creation, there was no time at all, for time cannot exist unless there is change. God Himself is changeless; otherwise you would find an infinite series of past events in His life, and we know that such an infinite series is impossible. So God is changeless, and hence, timeless prior to creation.

I think that the concept of the Trinity can help us to understand this. According to the Bible, God is not simply personal; He is tri-personal. Which is to say that in God's being there are three centers of self-consciousness instead of just one, as there is in a human being. Christians have tended to cloud the logical clarity of this concept by over-emphasizing the mysteriousness of the Trinity.

This doctrine in no way asserts that there are three Gods which are somehow one God. Rather it holds that, just as my being supports one center of self-consciousness, so God's being supports three centers of self-consciousness. So, although God may be truly said to be personal, it is not technically correct to say He is *a* person. God's nature enfolds three persons, that is, three centers of self-consciousness, each possessing the attributes of personhood: intellect, emotion and will. The three are co-equal but are called by the names "Father," "Son" and "Holy Spirit" because of their respective roles in the plan of man's salvation.

Before creation, the Father, Son and Holy Spirit existed in a perfect and changeless love relationship. God was not lonely before creation. In the tri-unity of His own being, He was enjoying the fullness of divine personal relationships with an eternal plan for the creation and salvation of human persons.

This plan was not decided on several eons ago. It is an eternal plan. The Bible says Christ "had been chosen by God before the creation of the world, and was revealed in these last days for your sake."[12] God arranged our salvation "according to His eternal purpose which He achieved through Christ Jesus our Lord."[13] Why did He do this? Not because He needed us but simply because of His overflowing grace and love.

So, in my opinion, God is timeless prior to creation, and He created time along with the world. From the point of creation on, God places Himself within time so that He can interact with the world He has created. The Bible hints at this when it says, "To the only God . . . be glory, majesty, dominion and authority, *before all time* and *now* and *forever.*"[14]

Someday God will be done with this creation. The universe will not, in fact, suffer heat death, for God will have finished with it by then. According to the New Testament, God Himself will intervene to bring about the end of the universe.[15] The Bible says:

> You, Lord, in the beginning created the earth,
>   and with Your own hands You made the
>   heavens.
> They will all disappear, but You will remain;
>   they will all grow old like clothes.
> You will fold them up like a coat,
>   and they will be changed like clothes.
> But You are always the same,
>   and You will never grow old.[16]

Thus we reach our conclusion: A personal creator of the universe exists, changeless and timeless prior to creation and in time subsequent to creation. This is the central idea of what theists mean by "God." In the concluding chapter, I want to draw some practical applications from this conclusion.

An Argument for God's Existence (3): The Personal Creator of the Universe

NOTES

*An
Argument
for God's
Existence (3):
The
Personal
Creator
of the
Universe*

1. David Hume to John Stewart, February, 1754, in *The Letters of David Hume*, 2 vols., ed. J. Y. T. Greig (Oxford: Clarendon Press, 1932), 1, p. 187.
2. C. D. Broad, "Kant's Mathematical Antinomies," *Proceedings of the Aristotelian Society*, 55 (1955), p. 10.
3. Zwart, *Time*, p. 240.
4. Anthony Kenny, *The Five Ways: St. Thomas Aquinas' Proofs of God's Existence* (New York: Schocken Books, 1969), p. 66.
5. Hubert Reeves, Jean Audouze, William A. Fowler and David N. Schramm, "On the Origin of Light Elements," *Astrophysical Journal*, 179 (1973), pp. 909-930.
6. Albert Einstein, *Out of My Later Years* (New York: Philosophical Library, 1950), p. 58.
7. One interesting exception appears to be the well-known astronomer Icko Iben, who in a popular article felt free to comment: ". . . Matter in the universe was once crammed together at extremely high densities and at temperatures in excess of 10 billion degrees. The fact that under such conditions most of the energy in the universe was in the form of electro-magnetic radiation (photons) gives added meaning to the phrase, 'And God said, "Let there be light." ' " (Icko Iben, Jr., "Globular Cluster Stars," *Scientific American*, July, 1970, p. 39.)
8. Fred Hoyle, *Astronomy Today* (London: Heinemann, 1975), p. 166.
9. Adrian Webster, "The Cosmic Background Radiation," *Scientific American*, August, 1974, p. 31.
10. J. V. Narlikar, "Singularity and Matter Creation in Cosmological Models," *Nature: Physical Science*, 242 (1973), p. 136. Cf. the judgment of the team who identified the microwave background radiation of the universe: ". . . In the framework of the conventional theory we cannot understand the origin of matter or of the universe." (R. H. Dicke, P. J. E. Peebles, P. G. Roll and D. T. Wilkinson, "Cosmic Black-Body Radiation," *Astrophysical Journal*, 142 (1965), p. 414.

11. James Barr, *Biblical Words for Time* (London: SCM Press, 1962), pp. 80, 145-147.
12. I Peter 1:20 (Today's English Version).
13. Ephesians 3:11 (TEV).
14. Jude 25 (Revised Standard Version).
15. Romans 8:21; II Peter 3:10-13; Revelation 20:11; 21:1.
16. Hebrews 1:10-12 (TEV).

An Argument for God's Existence (3): The Personal Creator of the Universe

CHAPTER

5

Knowing God

In reading books which purport to prove the existence of God, I have always felt a little "let down" when, after pages and pages of abstruse reasoning, the author triumphantly proclaims, "Therefore, God exists!" This conclusion, reached only after long and difficult argument, seemed so dry and academic that it failed really to touch me. Perhaps you feel the same way at this point.

Knowing God

May I suggest that there is a viable explanation for this? I think this situation results largely because the knowledge of God is very different from knowledge of any other object or subject. In the first place, there is a vast difference between knowing about God and knowing God. Most books on the subject will enable us to know a lot about God — His goodness, power, wisdom and so on — but they do not really tell us how to know God personally.[1] And to that extent they are incomplete.

The Bible makes it clear that mere knowledge *about* God is not sufficient for knowledge *of* God; apparently even the demons believe there is one God — and tremble with fear, because they do not experience God's salvation.[2] So it is quite possible to believe *that* God exists without believing *in* God, to know about God and yet not know God.

Many people believe that there is a God, but it is evident from their lives that they do not really know Him personally; if they did, their lives would be different. Because they know about God but do not know Him personally, He seems unreal to most people. For the same reason, little *Knowing* excitement is generated when one at last reaches *God* the conclusion, "Therefore, God exists!" This statement can give us some knowledge about God, but it cannot in itself help us to know God.

Then why have proofs at all? Simply because it is impossible to believe in God unless one first recognizes His existence; we cannot know God unless we first have some knowledge about God. So concluding that God exists is only the first step; I now want to explain how we may know Him. For the person who knows God personally, God is not the conclusion to a syllogism; He is a living reality in his life.

A second difference about the knowledge of God is that, unlike any other type of knowledge, it is conditioned by moral and spiritual factors. A wicked man may know geometry or even theology as well as a righteous man. But a wicked man cannot know God. The Bible makes it clear that God, being pure, cannot look upon evil;[3] evil is dispersed from His presence as darkness is from light. So knowing God involves moral and spiritual factors not involved in other types of knowledge.

A man who rebels at this will often believe the most ridiculous hypotheses rather than admit God's existence. In this he condemns himself, because the testimony of creation around him makes it evident that God exists:

> God punishes them because what men can know about God is plain to them. God Himself made it plain to them. Ever since God created the world, His invisible qualities, both His eternal power and His divine nature, have been clearly seen. Men can perceive them in the things that God has made. So they have no excuse at all![4]

Knowing God

Nevertheless, people will go to extreme lengths to explain away the evidence for the Bible message rather than accept it.

For that reason I find the arguments presented in the earlier chapters attractive: They leave the unbeliever a way of escape. If he wants to, he can always deny the universe was caused and assert that it sprang into being uncaused out of nothing. But if he does, of course, he exposes himself as interested only in an academic refutation of the proof and not in really discovering the truth about God or the universe; for as we noted, even skeptics like Hume considered it absurd that something could come to exist out of nothing and without a cause.

How does a person arrive at a personal knowledge of God? First and most important, he must seek God sincerely, with an open mind and an open heart. Then he must have some understanding of the following biblical concepts.

1. *God loves man and created him in such a way that man can know God.* Jesus taught that God loves the world He created and that He calls and draws men to a personal relationship with Himself.[5] He also taught that "God is Spirit. . . ."[6] In order to enable finite physical beings to gain a personal knowledge of an infi-

nite spiritual being, God created man in His personal image, with a spiritual dimension which gives him the capacity to know God in a way that mere animals cannot.[7] Of all the earthly creatures, man alone was created in such a way that he might know and commune with God and share His love.

Knowing God

2. *Man's evil destroys his spiritual capacity to know God*. By means of his free will, man rebels against God through evil thoughts and acts. The results of this rebellion are threefold:

(a) Man is spiritually dead and cut off from God. The Bible says, "The soul that sins shall die," and "the wages of sin is death."[8] Thus, man is "spiritually dead because of . . . disobedience and sins."[9] As a result, man is separated from God. The Bible says, "Your iniquities have made a separation between you and your God, and your sins have hid His face from you so that He does not hear;"[10] "All men have sinned and are far away from God's saving presence."[11] Thus, all men are cut off from God.

(b) Man is morally guilty before God. God expressed His own perfect moral nature in the Ten Commandments and implanted His moral law in the conscience and mind of each human being.[12] When man chooses evil, he violates God's moral law and becomes guilty before God. And because God is just, He must punish wrong; if He did not, He would not be good. This punishment is "eternal destruction and exclusion from the presence of the Lord."[13]

(c) Man himself cannot possibly reach God. It is impossible for man, spiritually dead and mor-

98

ally guilty before God, to reach God by his own efforts.

So often we hear it said that if we obey the Golden Rule or the Ten Commandments, or if our good works outbalance our bad works, God will accept us.

But the Bible teaches us, "No man is justified before God by the law" and "No human being will be justified in His sight by works of the law."[14] In fact, according to the New Testament, the law or the Ten Commandments were given, not as a means of reaching God by good works, but as a sort of moral yardstick to reveal to us how desperately short of God's righteousness we fall and to impel us to repent.[15]

Man could never do enough good works to earn salvation. The German philosopher Immanuel Kant argued that it would take an eternity for a man to measure up to God's moral law. And even then he would still stand guilty for all the wrong he had committed before he arrived at perfection.

Man, spiritually dead, can never fulfill God's moral law, and guilty before God, can never erase his guilt. No wonder the Bible claims that man in this condition is "without hope and without God."[16]

3. *Through Jesus Christ man can come to know God.* Before God ever created the universe, He knew that man would go astray, and He had already planned to rescue man from the hopeless condition into which he would plunge himself.

The second person of the Trinity, whom we call the Son, would take to Himself a human

Knowing God

nature and thereby "become" a man. By this I do not mean that God the Son ceased to be God; rather, Jesus was both fully man and fully God. Perhaps the best way to conceive this is to realize that the second center of self-consciousness in the Trinity *was* the mind of Jesus. Hence, Jesus was literally God incarnate, God "in the flesh" (from the Latin *in* + *carnis*, meaning "flesh").

Knowing God

On the cross, Jesus voluntarily took upon Himself the punishment for the sins of men, thus making possible the offer of forgiveness and pardon to whomever would receive it, and thereby healing the breach in the relationship between men and God. Jesus is therefore the solution to man's predicament:

(a) Through Jesus, man is spiritually born again and comes to know God. When a person becomes a Christian, the Holy Spirit comes into him and makes alive the dead spiritual dimension within man. As Jesus said, "No one can see the Kingdom of God unless he is born again. . . . A man is born physically of human parents, but he is born spiritually of the Spirit."[17] So man's spiritual capacity to know God is restored, and a new life begins; he is "born again."

(b) Through Jesus, man's guilt is forgiven. Over and over again the Bible proclaims this good news: On the cross, Jesus paid the penalty for sin that we deserved; He died in our place. We do not need to be punished for violating God's moral law, for God in the person of Jesus has paid the penalty Himself. As the Bible states, "There is therefore now no condemnation for those who are in Christ Jesus."[18]

(c) Through Jesus, man is brought back to God. Left to our own limited resources, we could never reach God, but Christ restores our broken relationship with God apart from any effort of our own. Thus, salvation is a free gift; we cannot earn it. The Bible explains:

Knowing God

> But when the kindness and love of God our Savior appeared, He saved us. It was not because of any good works that we ourselves had done, but because of His own mercy that He saved us through the washing by which the Holy Spirit gives us new birth and new life. For God abundantly poured out the Holy Spirit on us, through Jesus Christ our Savior, that by His grace we might be put right with God and come into possession of the eternal life we hope for.[19]

So, when a person is born again, he becomes spiritually alive and comes into a personal relationship with God. All his guilt is forgiven, and life starts all over again for him. And all this is a free gift of God made possible by Jesus' death in our place.

4. *Man comes to know God by receiving Jesus as his personal Savior and Lord.* The Bible says, "To all who received Him, who believed in His name, He gave power to become children of God; who were born, not . . . of man, but of God."[20] We receive Jesus by placing our faith or trust in Him. The Bible says:

> But now the righteousness of God has been manifested apart from law, . . . the righteousness of God through faith in Jesus Christ for all who believe. For there is no distinction; since all have sinned and fall short of the glory of God, they are

justified by His grace as a gift, through the redemption which is in Christ Jesus, whom God
put forward as an expiation by His blood, to be
received by faith.[21]

When we trust Jesus to be Savior and Lord of our
lives, the Holy Spirit actually comes into us, indwells us and gives us a fresh life with God.

*Knowing
God*

We can receive Jesus by personal invitation.
Jesus stands at the door of each of our lives,
seeking entrance. He says, "Behold, I stand at the
door and knock; if any one hears My voice and
opens the door, I will come in to him."[22] Receiving Jesus involves admitting that one is spiritually dead and guilty before God, turning to
God from one's evil thoughts and actions, and
asking Christ to come into one's life to forgive
one's sins, to give new spiritual life and to be the
Master of one's life.

Receiving Jesus is not necessarily an emotional experience, but neither is it enough to give
mere intellectual agreement to the contents of
this chapter. Rather, one simply and willingly
decides to turn over one's life to Jesus and let
Him be both Savior and Lord.

If you would sincerely like to know God in a
personal way, simply tell Him about it. You
might find it hard to know what to say, so here is
a suggested prayer:

> Lord Jesus, I really need You. I admit that I
> have wronged You, and right now, I turn from
> those wrongs and open the door of my life.
> Come into my life, forgive my sins and make me
> the person You created me to be. Thank You for
> hearing my prayer and coming into my life.

If you sincerely invited Christ into your life, you can know with confidence that He accepted your invitation. You may feel no different, but remember: You are saved through faith, not feelings.

I have seen grown men reduced to tears when they yielded to Christ, but I have seen others who have received Him with no emotional impact whatsoever. There are as many different experiences as there are personalities, but there is no necessary relationship between the emotionality of one's conversion and the vitality of one's subsequent walk with God. The crucial factor is not our emotions but the sincerity and depth of our trust.

Knowing God

When a person is born again into a personal relationship with God, several things immediately happen to him:

(a) He is indwelt by the Holy Spirit. According to the Bible, the Holy Spirit truly indwells every person who is born again.[23] Jesus taught that the Holy Spirit is the inner source of overflowing power in the life of a Christian.[24] A person who yields to the power and direction of the Holy Spirit is described as "filled with the Spirit."[25] (Compare our expressions "filled with anger" or "filled with jealousy," used to describe a person who is controlled by those emotions.) You will enjoy the full vitality of your relationship with God as you allow the indwelling Spirit of God to empower and direct you day by day.

(b) He becomes a child of God. While all men are God's creatures, only those who have been born again can truly be called His children.[26]

103

This is the greatest privilege anyone can have, to become an adopted brother or sister of Jesus, the true Son of God, and an heir of all the promised blessings of God.

It also means that we are part of a worldwide family of believers who know God and who are united with one another in His love. How wonderful to travel anywhere, even to nations of different languages, and to feel at once the love and openness of a total stranger who shares your commitment to Jesus!

(c) He is forgiven of all his evil thoughts and actions. When a person receives Christ, God not only wipes the slate clean but He also throws away the slate! He promises, "I will remember their sins no more."[27]

When a person receives Christ, he is instantaneously transferred from the realm of spiritual darkness to that of light. The Bible explains that God "has delivered us from the dominion of darkness and transferred us to the kingdom of His beloved Son, in whom we have redemption, the forgiveness of sins."[28] Therefore, since we have been saved from this darkness, it would be madness to go on living in it.[29]

Of course, a Christian will not suddenly live a perfect life, but he will no longer *practice* sin as a way of life.[30] When he does stumble and do wrong, he has the assurance that if he acknowledges his wrong, God will forgive and cleanse him from it.[31]

Now that God has delivered you from the darkness of evil, avoid it at all costs. Should you sense that you have displeased Him in some way, acknowledge it to Him immediately, confident that He loves and forgives you.

(d) He receives eternal life. When a person places his faith in Jesus and is born again, it is *eternal* life to which he is born.[32] According to the Bible, "God gave us eternal life, and this life is in His Son. He who has the Son has life; he who has not the Son of God has not life. I write this to you who believe in the name of the Son of God, that you may know that you have eternal life."[33] So the believer does not receive eternal life when he dies, but at the very moment he receives Christ.

Knowing God

When a believer dies physically, he goes at once to be with Christ.[34] When God terminates the present universe to usher in the new age, the believer will receive a body similar to that which Jesus had after His resurrection.[35] And so we shall always be with the Lord.

Therefore, you should live your life in light of eternity and invest your time and your talents in activities of eternal value. Consider the implications of this couplet: "Only one life — 'twill soon be past. / Only what's done for Christ will last."

There are so many other blessings that are yours in Christ that I cannot even begin to enumerate them. Like a spiritual baby beginning a new life, you have much to learn. To stimulate your spiritual growth, read your New Testament daily, talk to God often in prayer and find other Christians with whom you can share your Christian life. You may even wish to write the publisher of this book to request Christian literature to read.

I am thrilled for you, and I wish you *bon*

voyage! For you are beginning the most exciting adventure any human being can experience: knowing God through the Lord Jesus Christ.

Knowing God

NOTES

1. One highly recommended book is James I. Packer, *Knowing God*, (London: Hodder & Stoughton, 1973).
2. James 2:19 (Today's English Version)
3. Habakkuk 1:13.
4. Romans 1:19,20 (TEV).
5. John 6:37,40,44,47.
6. John 4:24 (TEV).
7. I Thessalonians 5:23.
8. Ezekiel 18:4; Romans 6:23 (Revised Standard Version).
9. Ephesians 2:1 (TEV).
10. Isaiah 59:2 (RSV).
11. Romans 3:23 (TEV).
12. Romans 1:12-16.
13. II Thessalonians 1:9 (RSV).
14. Galatians 3:11; Romans 3:20 (RSV).
15. Romans 5:20; 7:7-14; Galatians 3:21-24.
16. Ephesians 2:12 (TEV).
17. John 3:3,6 (TEV).
18. Romans 8:1 (RSV).
19. Titus 3:4-7 (TEV).
20. John 1:12,13 (RSV).
21. Romans 3:21-25 (RSV).
22. Revelation 3:20 (RSV).
23. Romans 8:9.
24. John 7:37-39; Acts 1:8.
25. Ephesians 5:18.
26. John 1:12,13; Romans 8:14-17; Galatians 3:25-4:7.
27. Hebrews 8:12b (RSV).
28. Colossians 1:13,14 (RSV).
29. Romans 6:12-23.
30. I John 3:6,9.
31. I John 1:9.
32. John 3:16,36; 6:40; 10:27,28.
33. I John 5:11-13 (RSV).
34. II Corinthians 5:6-9; Philippians 1:23.
35. I Corinthians 15:20, 42-57; Philippians 3:20,21.

Knowing God